You Might Be A Douchebag

by Joe Bartnick

Illustrated by Steve Baduce
Produced and Edited by Vinnie Corbo

Published by Volossal Publishing
www.volossal.com

Copyright © 2011
ISBN 978-0-9909727-9-2

This book may not be reproduced or resold in whole or in part
through print, electronic or any other medium. All rights reserved.

Dedication

To the Buns and the Boo,
my Goddesses.

Special Thanks to Vinnie Corbo for making it happen.

Introduction

Nobody ever thinks they're a douchebag. It's easy to point to someone else and proclaim them to be a douchebag but when it comes to douchebag self awareness, most of us exist in a state of total douchebag denial.

That's why I wrote this book. I want to help you avoid being a douchebag.

Simply put, a douchebag is someone who is not cool. Everyone wants to be cool. No one wants to be a douchebag...well almost no one. So, I'm here to help. I've put together a collection of behaviors that will let you know if you might be a douchebag. I've even added illustrations. Because you might be a douchebag without even knowing it.

Now, some of you might get mad when you realize you've been acting like a douchebag. But remember, we all act like douchebags sometimes, but hopefully not all of the time.

So don't get mad; get cool.

- Joe Barnick

You Might Be A Douchebag

The Standards

You Might Be A Douchebag

If you give yourself a nickname.

If you have a badge and no gun.

If you don't think farts are hilarious.

If your name starts with DJ.

If you start a conversation at the urinal.

If you don't buy enough booze for your party.

If your Christmas tree isn't green.

If you complain a massage is too rough.

If you take baths.

If you don't think AC/DC rules.

Cars and Driving

If you let your woman drive, ever,
and you're not drunk.

If you can't parallel park.

If you drive slow in the carpool lane.

If you stop at yellow lights.

If you flash your high beams at someone.

If you use medium gas.

If your car payment is bigger than your rent.

If you stick your car out in the road before you pullout.

If you drive with your lights on in the daytime.

If you put a bumper sticker on a Cadillac.

If you have a dirty windshield.

If you don't wave when someone is nice to you on the road.

If the only fluid you put in your car is gas.

If you can't change a tire.

If you have a "I'd rather be…" bumper sticker.

If you have a "My other car is a…" bumper sticker.

If you put your religion on a bumper sticker.

If you have a decorative license plate.

If you block traffic waiting for a parking space.

Eating and Drinking

If you put sprouts on a sandwich.

If you use chopsticks at home.

If you go to a restaurant
to have Happy Birthday sung to you.

If you don't have a "go to" shot.

If you tell the waitress you're a big tipper.

If you ask for a beer list then order Coors light.

If you can't finish your drink.

If you peel the label off a beer bottle.

If you get a fruit plate instead of fries.

If you dissect the bill.

If you tip with change.

If you change your order when some else pays.

If you think 15% is a good tip.

If you customize your order at a fast food chain.

If you drink a soy anything.

If your entrée salad has no meat on it.

If you have to open the door at a drive thru.

If you bring Hard Lemonade to a party and you're not banging a high school chick.

If you drink with a straw.

If you get a soda with a water cup.

If you get a side of Ranch dressing with everything.

If you eat pizza with a flavored crust.

If you call a burrito a wrap.

If you take the nacho chip with all the cheese on it.

If you buy a small beer at the game.

You Might Be A Douchebag

Sports and The Gym

If you spike on a girl in Volleyball.

If your football team is the Cowboys and you don't live in Texas.

If you fight a kid for a foul ball.

If you don't like hockey
because you don't understand it.

If the only football game you watch all year
is the Super Bowl.

If you take your shirt off at the game
in freezing weather.

If you think every game is fixed.

If you think steroids ruin sports.

If you wave to a television camera during a game.

If you get dressed up to ride a bike.

If you bring a notebook to the gym.

If every time you miss a shot,
you claim you got fouled.

If you take a charge in a rec league.

If you take a slapshot in a beer league.

If you bring out the bridge when playing pool.

If your darts don't stick in the board.

If you wear weight lifting gloves.

If you use the cardio machine right next to someone.

If you do lunges at the gym.

If you leave before the game is over.

If you leave your seat during game action.

If you shout before the National Anthem is over.

If you put your own name on a hockey sweater.

If you don't touch your chest with the bar
when you bench press.

If the first thing you put on in a locker room isn't your underwear.

More Standards

You Might Be A Douchebag

If you talk smack in an opposing stadium.

If you talk about women's basketball.

If you fall for the (let's share two entrees).

If your car floor is a garbage can.

If you keep your Christmas lights up all year.

If you use the word cute.

If you buy snacks from the bathroom attendants.

If you lend out a book and expect it back.

If you don't thank the door holder.

If you break your hand punching an inanimate object.

If you have a clock you know has the wrong time.

If you write your screen play at Starbucks.

If you invite people to play games with you on the internet.

If you use the air dryer in the Men's room.

If you don't put your shopping cart back.

If you don't flush a public toilet.

If you think leaving a gift in the store bag is the same as wrapping it.

If you name a kid after a famous person you don't know.

If you don't hand out candy on Halloween.

If your profile picture is empty.

Partying and Strip Clubs

You Might Be A Douchebag

If you bring a woman to Vegas.

If you play slot machines.

If you've ever felt bad for the stripper.

If you try to remember the strippers real name.

If you come home with glitter all over you.

If you sit right next to a guy getting a lap dance.

If you talk to another guy while he's getting a lap dance.

If you put drinks on a pool table.

If you eat at the strip club.

If you think the stripper likes you.

If you don't tip at a strip club's "snatch" bar.

If you smoke everyday and never buy a pack.

If you put tobacco in your joints.

If you complain about the butane in lighters.

If you never change your bong water.

If you use diet sodas for mixers.

Fashion

If you can't tie a tie.

If your shoes or wallet have Velcro.

If you wear sandals and pants.

If you're still getting a barbed wire tattoo.

If your t-shirt sparkles.

If you wear a scarf and its not cold outside.

If you put highlights in your hair.

If you wear your cap off to the side.

If you're not in a tribe but you have the tattoo.

If you wear socks at the beach.

If you keep sunglasses on top of your head after dark.

If you wear more jewelry than a chick.

If your bracelet isn't made of metal.

If you have a fake tux t-shirt.

If you wear tennis shoes with a suit.

If you work at making your hair look messy.

If you wear a visor; ever.

Parenting

If you dress your twins exactly the same.

If you keep your kid on a leash.

If you make your kids wear a helmet for everything.

If you don't make your kids say
"please" and "thank you" for everything.

If you smack your kids in public.

If all your kid's names start with the same letter.

If you shave your kid's head.

If you let your kids win every time.

If you let your kid walk up the slide as other kids are going down.

If you force healthy snacks on your kids.

If you take Little League sports seriously.

If you do their homework for them.

If you drive them to school when they can walk.

If you jump the Pick-Up / Drop-Off line at school.

If you tell people how to parent and don't have kids.

You Might Be A Douchebag

Pets

You Might Be A Douchebag

If you walk a dog that doesn't come up to your knee.

If you dress up your dog in team colors.

If you care about animals more than people.

If your dog has a real person's name.

If you think rodents are pets.

If your cause célèbre is defending pitbulls.

If a truck stop toilet is cleaner than your fish tank.

If your fish tank has only one fish.

If you let your dog eat from the table.

You Might Be A Douchebag

Relationships

You Might Be A Douchebag

If you split a check with a date.

If you ride in a handsome cab.

If you hold hands while sitting down in public.

If you bring your own putter on a miniature golf date.

If you get a doggy bag.

If you don't wait to make sure she gets in safe.

If you don't hold the door for a woman.

If you make a girl watch you eat.

If you go on coffee dates.

If you use coupons on a date.

If you make out at the bar.

If you make her find out what the noise is.

If you videotape sex with someone
you're not supposed to be with.

If you say the wrong name in bed.

If you break up before holidays or birthdays
to save money.

If you don't walk her to her car.

If you go antiquing.

If you let your woman control the remote.

If you get married in nature.

If you leave more than 3 CD's at her house.

If you work on your honeymoon.

If you surprise your girl at work.

If you go to a shower of any kind.

If you move in together to save money on rent.

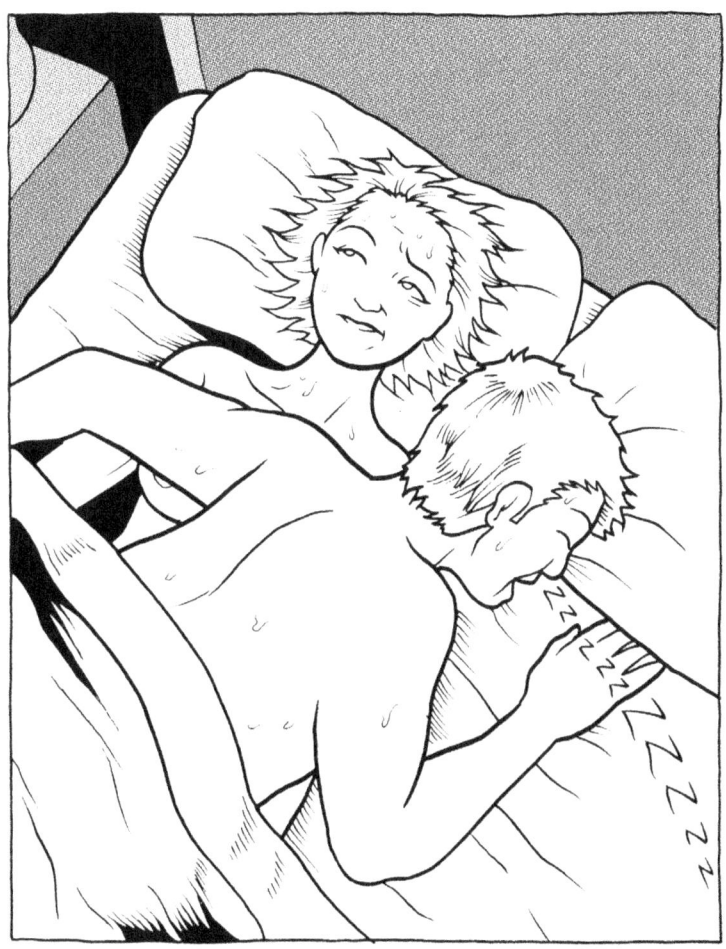

If you fall asleep before she has an orgasm.

If you wear the same outfits.

If you think hanging with the girls
gives you a chance at group sex.

If you don't let her have a ladies night out.

If you check in with her.

If you tell her you love her and you don't.

If you buy her an appliance as a gift.

If you buy her day old flowers because they're cheaper.

If you give her a homemade gift.

If you share intimate moments on the internet.

If you think blowjobs are cheating.

You Might Be A Douchebag

Bonus Douchebags

You Might Be A Douchebag

Golf

If you don't give your friend a mulligan.

If you take two mulligans.

If you don't give yourself a better lie when no one is looking.

If you take too many practice swings.

If you take forever looking for your ball.

If you watch golf on TV.

If you won't let someone play through.

If every time you talk about golf,
you swing an imaginary club.

If your putter looks like it's from outer space.

If you think golf is a sport.

Travel

If your carry-on is bigger than a Japanese car.

If you bring a guitar on an airplane.

If you eat the eggs at the free continental breakfast.

If you have a window seat and get up more than once.

If you say more than three sentences to the person next to you on a plane.

Sucker Born Every Minute

If you buy a time share.

If you take the condo tour on vacation.

If you buy anything on TV for ...95.

If you get a caricature of yourself.

If you help someone move by yourself.

Concerts

If you want people at a concert in front of you to sit down.

If you clap to the music at a concert.

If you get lawn seats.

If you buy a bootleg t-shirt in the parking lot.

If you sing a song you don't know all the words to.

Super Bonus Douchebags

If you inhale cigars.

If you show up to a party or someone's house empty handed.

If you serve tap water.

If you make people take their shoes off in your house.

If your movie quotes don't come from either The Godfather or Goodfellas.

You Might Be A Douchebag

If you read this entire book at the store for free.

You Might Be A Douchebag

About The Author

Joe Bartnick was born in Pittsburgh where he learned his love of eating, drinking and sports. He started doing stand up comedy in San Francisco in the late 90's. Joe progressed from playing coffee shops , bars and Laundromats to being a regular a the World Famous Punchine. From there Joe has performed all over North America in such prestigious places as the Warfield, the Wiltern, Heinz Hall and the Chicago Theater. Joe did a closing set on AXS Tv's Live from Gotham.

Joe has appeared on several television shows including the ESPY's and the NFL on Fox. His hockey column can be seen on PunchDrunk.com and 2minute minor.com

Joe can be heard talking hockey on the Sideshow Network's *Puck Off* all year round and on WDVE during the season. He talks everything else on All Thing's Comedy's Insensitivity Training.

In 2014-2015 Joe can be seen on Bill Burr's *All in Tour*.

Publisher's Note

While the jokes in this book are based off events and experiences in Joe Bartnick's life, they are not about any specific individual or individuals. This book is intended purely for entertainment purposes.

Other Books From Volossal Publishing

Is Your Boyfriend Really Your Girlfriend?
Fetish and You
Sex, Fetish and Him
A Boy In Hiding
Tamales For Gringos
Cartoons That Will Send Me Straight To Hell
The Astrology Sex Diet
Jesus, Hitler, Manson and Me
The El
You've Got The Balls, Use Them!
Confessions of a Fat Player
Feeding The Beast
Why Not If It Works

Volossal Publishing
www.volossal.com

Joe Bartnick
www.joebartnick.com

You Might Be A Douchebag

www.ingramcontent.com/pod-product-compliance
Lightning Source LLC
LaVergne TN
LVHW051608070426
835507LV00021B/2839